Table of Contents

INTRODUCTION

African-American cookbooks, also known as “soul foods,” are often labeled as “poor food choices” because most use plant-based ingredients.However, that is completely inaccurate because you can find a wide range of irresistible delicious foods in the books below. And if you want to try cooking some African American dishes at home.Here are some African American cookbooks for you. Let these books help you recreate authentic African American cuisine.

Recipes

Garlic-Stuffed Chicken

Ingredients

- 2 cups water 8 cloves garlic, unpeeled
- 6 tablespoons chopped fresh parsley, divided
- 1 teaspoon grated lemon zest
- 1 teaspoon Mrs. Dash (or other sodium-free seasoning)

• 4 boneless chicken breasts, with skin (4-ounces each)

• ¼ cup reduced-sodium chicken broth

• 2 tablespoons fresh lemon juice in a small saucepan, bring water to a boil.

Instructions

• Add garlic; cook for 10 minutes.Drain garlic, peel and cut into thin slices. In a small bowl, combine garlic, ½ cup of chopped parsley, lemon zest, and seasoning.Mix well.

• Loosen skin from each chicken breast to form a pocket.Place about 1 teaspoon of garlic mixture under skin of each breast.Heat a large nonstick skillet over medium-high heat.Add chicken skin-side down; cook until golden, about 4 minutes. Turn chicken; reduce heat to medium.

• Cover and cook until no longer pink in center, about 10 to 12 minutes.Transfer chicken to a plate.Wipe any fat away from the skillet. Add remaining chopped parsley, broth, and lemon juice to pan.Bring to a boil; cook for 1 minute.Spoon mixture over chicken.

Makes 4 servings

Salmon Patties

If you don't have fresh bread crumbs on hand, you can substitute soup crackers with unsalted tops.

Ingredients

- 2 cans of pink salmon
- 2 eggs
- 1 cup fresh bread crumbs
- 1 tablespoon Mrs. Dash seasoning (or other sodium-free seasoning)
- Non-stick cooking spray

Instructions

- Pick any bones out of the salmon. In a mixing bowl, beat egg and add seasoning, bread crumbs and salmon.Gently mix until just combined.

• Divide the mixture into four parts. Roll into balls and flatten the balls into patties.

• Coat the bottom of a non-stick pan with a generous amount of non-stick cooking spray and heat the pan over medium heat.Cook the patties in the hot pan about 3 to 5 minutes on each side, until golden brown.

Makes 4 patties

Quick Tuna Casserole

This is easy to make and tasty! You can substitute any low-sodium "cream of" soup for the mushroom soup in this recipe (cream of celery, for example.) Also, if you don't have bread crumbs on hand, you can substitute soup crackers with unsalted tops.

Ingredients

• 1 quart water

• 5 ounce package wide egg noodles

• 10 ounce can of low-fat, low-sodium cream of mushroom soup

• 1/3 cup skim milk

- 1 can (6.5 ounces) of tuna packed in water
- 1 cup frozen green peas
- 1 cup fresh bread crumbs

Instructions

- Preheat oven to 350 degrees.
- Bring 1 quart of water to a boil in a large pot and cook the egg noodles in the water for 2 minutes.Then, cover the pot, remove from heat and let stand for 10 minutes.
- In the meantime, mix the soup and milk together in a bowl.Combine tuna and peas with the mixture and pour into a 1-quart casserole dish. Drain the noodles well and combine with the tuna mixture.Sprinkle the top with bread crumbs.
- Bake for 30 minutes.

Makes 6 servings

One Pot Pasta

Be sure to use a non-stick pan for this recipe and coat it well with non-stick cooking spray.Otherwise, the pasta will stick to the bottom.

- 1 teaspoon olive oil
- ½ cup sliced onion
- 1 cup fresh mushrooms, sliced 2 lbs (about 3 large) tomatoes, peeled and chopped
- 1 can (8 ounces) tomato puree without salt
- 1 cup water
- 2 teaspoons dried basil
- 1 teaspoon white sugar
- ¼ teaspoon garlic powder
- ¼ teaspoon black pepper
- 8 ounces macaroni

Instructions

• Spray a large non-stick cooking skillet with non-stick cooking spray. Add oil and heat over medium flame. Add onion and mushrooms.

• Cook, stirring frequently, for 3 to 5 minutes until tender. Add tomatoes, tomato puree, water, sugar and spices to the skillet. When mixture begins to boil, stir in the pasta.

• Cover, reduce heat to medium-low and simmer for 20 minutes.Stir the mixture every 4 to 5 minutes while cooking.

Makes 4 servings

Scrumptious Meat Loaf

Ingredients

• 1 lb ground beef, extra lean

• 1/2 cup tomato paste (4 ozs)

• 1/4 cup onion, chopped

• 1/4 cup green peppers

• 1/4 cup red peppers

• 1 cup tomatoes, fresh, blanched, chopped

- 1/2 tsp mustard, low sodium
- 1/4 tsp ground black pepper
- 1/2 tsp hot pepper, chopped
- 2 cloves garlic, chopped
- 2 stalks scallion, chopped
- 1/2 tsp ginger, ground
- 1/8 tsp nutmeg, ground
- 1 tsp orange rind, grated
- 1/2 tsp thyme, crushed
- 1/4 cup bread crumbs, finely grated

Instructions

- Mix all ingredients together.
- Place in 1-pound loaf pan (preferably a pan with a drip rack) and bake covered at 350° F for 50 minutes.
- Uncover pan and continue baking for 12 minutes.

Makes 6 servings

Chicken Diane

Ingredients

• 1 teaspoon olive oil

• 4 skinless chicken breast halves with bone (about 2 ¼ pounds)

• 2 green onions, chopped

• ½ cup chopped fresh parsley

• 1/3 cup reduced-sodium chicken broth

• 1 tablespoon apple juice

• 1 ½ teaspoons cornstarch

• 1 teaspoon Dijon mustard

• 1 teaspoon Mrs. Dash or other sodium-free seasoning

• ½ tablespoon unsalted butter

• 1 tablespoon fresh lemon juice

Instructions

• In a large nonstick skillet, heat oil over medium heat. Add chicken, meaty-side down; cook until browned, about 8 minutes. Turn the chicken; cover and cook until no longer peak near the bone, about 12 minutes.

• While chicken is cooking, in a blender, process green onions, parsley, broth, apple juice, cornstarch, mustard, and seasoning until smooth.

• Transfer chicken to a serving platter. Add margarine and broth mixture to skillet.Cook until slightly thickened, about 2 minutes.Remove from heat; stir in lemon juice. Spoon sauce over chicken and serve immediately. Makes 4 servings

Turkey Sausage Stuffed Collard Green Wraps

Who knew that collard greens could be enjoyed in a variety of ways?! These Turkey Sausage Stuffed Collard Green Wraps are a complete game changer! They make a deliciously, healthy meal or a great appetizer for your next party!!

Ingredients

• 6 large collard green leaves washed and stems removed

- 1 lb ground turkey sausage
- 1 tbsp olive oil
- ¾ cups cooked white rice
- 1 yellow bell pepper sliced
- 1 tbsp fresh red chili pepper diced
- 1 red bell pepper sliced
- 2 tsp fresh or dried rosemary
- 2 tsp garlic powder
- 2 tsp seasoning salt
- Salt/pepper to taste
- Optional: 6 tbsp shredded mozzarella cheese

Instructions

- Preheat oven to 350 degrees. Lightly grease a shallow baking dish
- In a large skillet, on medium heat, cook turkey sausage. Add in diced chili pepper.Be sure to break up sausage when cooking. When sausage is

thoroughly cooked, remove sausage from skillet and set aside.Season with salt/pepper to taste.

• In the same skillet, on medium heat, add olive oil, yellow and red bell pepper.Cook until veggies are tender.Season with rosemary, garlic powder, and seasoning salt. Set aside.

• On a flat surface, arrange collard green leaves and evenly distribute sausage mixture, bell pepper mixture, and rice.Sprinkle a tbsp of shredded cheese on each if desired.

• Carefully roll wraps, making sure that the stuffing does not fall out. Place each wrap in a shallow baking dish and bake for about 10 minutes, until collard greens are slightly tender.

• When done, remove from baking dish and serve.

• Enjoy!

Makes 6 Servings

Creole Seafood Courtbouillon

The fish is nestled in a bubbly creole tomato sauce seasoned with the trinity, roux, seafood stock and a splash of white wine. But, it does not stop there. Luckily I had some blue crabs in the freezer and threw some of them in along with some shrimp. The perfect meal. Any fish can be used. I love using red fish but only found red snapper out here, so feel free to use whatever you are able to find in your area.

Instructions

- 1 whole red fish or fish of choise (2-3lbs)
- 1 1/2 teaspoon kosher salt
- Fresh cracked black pepper
- 1/2 cup roux
- 1 cup onions, chopped
- 1 cup green bell peppers, chopped
- 1/2 cup celery, chopped
- 4 cloves garlic, minced
- 3 blue crabs, cut in half
- 1/2 cup white wine
- 1 teaspoon creole seasoning

• 1 teaspoon red pepper flakes

• 1 28oz can of diced tomatoes

• 2 cups shrimp stock

• 2 bay leaves

• 1 tablespoon Worcesterhire sauce

• 1 sprig of tarragon or fresh thyme

• 1 pound shrimp, peeled and deveined

• 1 pint of oysters (optional)

• 2 bunches of green onions, chopped

• 1 lemon cut in half

Instructions

• Preheat oven to 350 degrees. Score fish on both sides and then season with salt and black pepper and place in a roasting pan.

• In a pan over medium heat, add your roux. Add the onions, bell peppers and celery. Cook for 5-6 minutes and then add garlic, blue crabs, wine, creole seasoning and red pepper flakes. Cook for 3-4 minutes.

• Increase the heat and add the can of tomatoes, shrimp stock, tarragon, and bay leaves. Bring to a boil and season with salt, pepper and Worcestershire sauce.

• Pour creole sauce over the redfish and cover with foil. Bake for 35-40 minutes. Remove foil and add shrimp and oysters (if using) around fish and bake uncovered for another 15-20 minutes.

• Serve with rice and green onions.

Nigerian Jollof Rice

What is Jollof Rice

Jollof rice is a West African staple recipe that starts with a simple red stew as the flavor base.The rice cooks in this combination of fresh vegetables, aromatics, and spices, plus a few other add ins

Ingredients

• 7 tomatoes cut into chunks

• 1 red bell pepper seeded and cut into chunks

- ½ white onion cut into chunks
- 4 habanero or scotch bonnet peppers use fewer or more depending on your preference
- ½ cup water
- 8 cups parboiled rice rinsed
- ¼-1/3 cup vegetable oil
- 8 ounces tomato sauce
- 4-6 ounces tomato paste
- 4 cubes chicken and/or beef buillon crushed
- 3 cups chicken and or beef stock
- 2 teaspoons powdered white pepper
- 2 teaspoons curry powder
- 1 teaspoon powdered bay leaf
- 1 teaspoon powdered thyme
- Sea salt to taste

Instructions

• Add tomatoes, onion, red bell pepper, and habanero peppers to a blender with ½ cup of water then blend until completely liquefied and uniform (about 2 minutes).

• Meanwhile, rinse the parboiled rice in plenty of warm water then drain.

• Add rice and vegetable oil to a large pot over medium flame, followed by blended tomato mixture, tomato paste and sauce, chicken and beef stocks, crushed bouillon, white pepper, curry powder, powdered bay leaf, powdered thyme, and sea salt.Stir everything together until uniform.

• Cook for about 40 minutes or until rice is cooked through and all liquid has dissipated, stir (to help prevent sticking and burning) and taste-test the liquid and rice as you go.

• It may be necessary to add more liquid along the way to prevent the rice at the bottom from burning excessively (see recipe notes). The bottom layer of rice in a pot of jollof rice often burns, which is where the smoky flavor comes from. Some believe that the rice tastes best when this happens. As you stir the rice and expose any burnt portions, you can simply discard them if you don't want them in the rice.

Recipe Notes

• Spice measurements are to taste, which is why tasting as you go is so important.

• Jollof rice burns quickly so it is best to use a non-stick pot and cook over medium heat.

• As the rice cooks and liquid dissipates, you may find it necessary to add additional ingredients according to your preference:

1. More Oil For Moisture

2. More Stock Or Bouillon For Flavor

3. More Tomato Paste Or Sauce For Color

4. Sea Salt To Your Taste

Pie Crust

These mini fried peach pies are crispy, flaky and delicious.They are filled with a cinnamon peach filling then fried to perfection.

Ingredients

- 2¼ cup all-purpose flour
- ½ teaspoon salt
- 1 tablespoon sugar
- ½ teaspoon baking powder
- ½ cup of butter (1 stick), grated
- ½ cup of water, cold
- 1 tablespoon vinegar

Filling

- 2 peaches, peeled, pitted, and diced
- ¼ cup brown sugar
- 1 tablespoon granulated sugar
- ½ teaspoon cinnamon

- ⅛ teaspoon nutmeg
- Pinch of salt
- 1 tablespoon flour
- 1 tablespoon water
- 1 tablespoon butter
- 1 cup canola oil

Instructions

Pie Crust:

- In a large bowl combine flour, salt, sugar, and baking powder.
- Add butter and coat flour until tiny bits of butter is incorporated throughout the flour.
- Add vinegar to water.
- Add water to flour mixture until the dough comes together.
- Set mixture in the refrigerator.

Filling:

• In a small bowl, mix the first 5 ingredients. Set aside.

• In a small bowl, mix the flour and water.

• In a medium-sized heavy skillet over medium heat, melt butter.

• Add peaches and stir.

• Sprinkle sugar mixture over peaches and stir.

• Add flour/water mixture (slurry) and stir.

• Cover and cook about 7 minutes until tender.

• Remove from heat and let cool.

Assemble:

• In batches roll out dough to ⅛ inch thick cut out thirteen or fourteen 4 inch circles. Place about a tablespoon of the cooled filling a little of center on the circle. Fold over the dough then crimp with a fork.Repeat until done.

• In a large sided skillet, heat about one inch of oil over medium-high heat.In batches making sure not to overcrowd the skillet fry pies until they are golden brown, about 5 minutes. Place on a plate lined with 2 paper towels

Recipe Type: Dessert

Orange Bundt Cake

This Bundt cake is flavored with orange juice and zest to fill it with citrus flavor.It's then coated in a vanilla glaze for a picture-perfect dessert.

Ingredients

• Nonstick cooking spray

• 2 sticks (1 cup) unsalted butter, at room temperature

• 2 cups granulated sugar

• 1 tablespoon orange zest (from about 1 medium orange)

• 4 large eggs

• 3 cups all-purpose flour

• 1 tablespoon plus 1/2 teaspoon baking powder

• 1/2 teaspoon salt

• 1/2 cup whole milk

• 1/2 cup (preferably fresh squeezed) orange juice

Vanilla Glaze

• 1 cup confectioners' sugar

• 2 tablespoons whole milk

• 1/2 teaspoon vanilla extract

Instructions

For the Orange Bundt Cake

• Preheat oven to 350°F. Spray a 10-inch fluted mold (Bundt) pan with nonstick cooking spray.

• In the bowl of a stand mixer fitted with a paddle attachment (or with a hand mixer), cream together the butter, sugar, and orange zest on medium-high to high speed until pale and fluffy, 3 to 5 minutes. Add in the eggs, one at a time, scraping down the sides of the bowl with a rubber spatula.

• Sift together the flour, baking powder, and salt. Alternately add the dry and wet ingredients to the butter mixture, starting and ending with the dry ingredients. (If using a stand mixer, it's best to finish by hand with a rubber spatula to make sure all of the ingredients are evenly incorporated without over-mixing.)

• Pour the batter into the prepared pan and bake until a toothpick inserted in the cake comes out clean, about 45 minutes.

• Let cool in the pan for a little while before turning out onto a baking rack to cool completely.

For The Vanilla Glaze

• Stir all of the ingredients together until smooth.Drizzle over the cooled cake.

Prawns in Spicy Curry Cream Sauce

This is an easy weeknight dinner dish with succulent shrimp served with a creamy, spicy sauce with a mix of masala, turmeric, scotch bonnet and creamy coconut milk.

Ingredients:

• 2 pounds jumbo shrimp

• 3 tablespoons olive oil

- 3 cloves garlic, chopped
- 2 shallots, chopped
- 3 scotch bonnet peppers, chopped
- 1/2 teaspoon marsala
- 1/2 cup dry white wine
- 1 tablespoon lemon juice
- 1/2 cup coconut milk (make your own)
- 2 ripe mangoes, peeled, pitted and sliced thin (optional)
- 1/4 teaspoon saffron

Instructions:

- Heat oil
- Add shallots, pepper, marsala, turmeric, saffron
- Saute for 2 mins
- Add wine, lemon juice, and shrimp
- Simmer until cooked through (about 4 mins)
- Remove shrimp with slotted spoon

- Lower sauce to simmer until reduced to half
- Add milk and simmer until thickened. Do not let milk burn
- Serve shrimp with mangoes over rice and a serving of spicy sauce.

Makes 4-6 Servings

Buttermilk Biscuits with Fried Chicken and Tabasco Honey

Ingredients

- 3 1/2 cups flour
- 1 1/4 cup buttermilk
- 1 cup unsalted butter
- 1/2 tsp baking soda
- 2 1/2 tsp baking powder
- 2 tsp koser salt
- 4 tsp sugar

Instructions

• Cube butter into half inch pieces and place it in the freezer for 10 minutes. While the butter is in the freezer mix together the flour, salt, sugar, baking powder, and baking soda.

• With a pastry cutter, fork, or your hands mix the butter into the dry ingredients. Mix until your dough gets to the points where there is large excess of dry flour remaining.

• Pour in about a cup of the buttermilk and begin to mix it (by hand) into the dry ingredients. Add the additional 1/4 cup of buttermilk as needed until there is no dry flour left.Work the dough into a ball and place it onto a floured surface.

• Roll/pat the dough out into a square about 1" thick. Cut the square into four pieces and stack them on top of each other.Again roll/pat the dough into a square about 1" thick.

• Cut out your biscuits and transfer them into the freezer to firm up for about 15 minutes.Preheat oven to 425 F.

• Remove biscuits from the freezer and rub the tops of them with melted butter. Place them into the oven and bake for 22-25 minutes.

• After you take the biscuits out of the oven baste with lots of butter and enjoy them jelly, sausage gravy, fried chicken, or my personal favorite fig jam.

Notes

Biscuits can be frozen for up to a month. Just add 5-10 minutes additional to the cooking time.

Makes 12 Biscuits

Southern Style Mac and Cheese + Bhm Virtual Potluck

It sure doesn't get any better than this southern style mac and cheese. Rich in flavor, extra cheesy, and true to its classic southern roots with those crispy brown edges.

Ingredients

• 1 lb (1 box) elbow macaroni

• 1 stick unsalted butter

• 2 eggs

• 2 cups half and half

• 2 cups (16 oz block) extra sharp cheddar cheese, grated

• 2 cups (16 oz block) Monterey Jack cheese, grated

• 8 oz block Velveeta cheese

• 1 tsp seasoned salt

• 1/4 tsp ground mustard

• 1/4 tsp paprika

• 1/4 tsp garlic powder

• A pinch of fresh cracked black pepper

Instructions

• Preheat the oven to 350°F and butter a 9X13-inch baking dish.

• Hand-grate the extra sharp cheddar and Monterey Jack cheese and set aside.

• In a large sauce pan, bring water to a boil.

• Cook macaroni according to package directions (al dente).

• Drain water from macaroni and return to pot.

• While macaroni is still hot, add butter, and stir until butter has melted completely and fully coated the macaroni.

• In a medium sized bowl, combine the eggs, half and half, and all of the spices together.Whisk until fully incorporated.

• Add egg mixture to macaroni pot as well as the majority of the grated cheese, leaving a few handfuls for topping. Cube the Velveeta and add in as well. Stir to mix well. The mixture will look creamy and all the cheese should have melted. If you see a few chunks of cheese unmelted, this is ok as any remains will melt away in the oven.

• Pour contents into prepared baking dish and top with any remaining grated cheese.

• Bake for 35-40 minutes or until top of mac and cheese is lightly golden brown.

• Let cool before serving and enjoy!

Makes 10 – 12 Servings

Olive Oil Braised Collard Greens

Ingredients

• 1/2 cup olive oil (and more for drizzling)

• 8 garlic cloves, sliced thin

• 1/2 teaspoon red pepper flakes

• 2 bunches collard greens, torn into 2" pieces (ribs & stem removed)

• Kosher salt

• Black pepper

• 1 tablespoon (plus an extra splash) apple cider vinegar

• Pinch of sugar

Instructions

• Heat 1/2 cup oil in large pot (or Dutch oven) over medium heat.

• Cook garlic and red pepper flakes often until garlic is a deep golden brown. Be careful not to burn the garlic.

• Add greens to the pot, one handful at a time, making sure each group is wilted before adding the next handful; season with salt and pepper.

• Add a cup of water* then bring to a simmer. Reduce the heat and allow the greens to simmer gently.

• Cover and cook, stirring occasionally until the greens are a deep dark green color and tender (about 1-1 1/2 hours).

• Let the greens cool slightly then add in the vinegar and sugar.

• Transfer to a serving dish then drizzle more olive oil on top.

Crawfish Etouffee

Crawfish Etouffee is a quintessential Cajun and Creole dish.It's a thick and hearty dish full of plump crawfish and jam packed with flavor

Ingredients:

• 1 stick of butter or 1/4 cup of vegetable oil

• 1/3 cup of all-purpose flour

• 1 TBS Cajun seasoning

• 1 tsp garlic powder

• Louisiana Hot Sauce to taste

• 2 cups seafood or chicken stock

• 1 cup of green onions, chopped

• 2 stalks of celery, chopped

• 1 small to medium onion, chopped

• 2 cloves of garlic, chopped

• 1/4 cup of parsley, chopped

• 2-3 cups of Crawfish tails

• Cooked white rice

Instructions

• Melt butter or heat vegetable oil in a cast iron skillet or heavy bottom pot.

• Slowly whisk in flour over a medium to low heat continuously until the roux is a chocolate brown. This will take 10-12 minutes.

• Mix in vegetables (onion, garlic, celery, and green onions) and cook until tender.This will take 3 minutes.Reserve some green onions for garnish.

• Add crawfish tails and season with Cajun seasoning and garlic powder.

• Add stock and combine all of the ingredients.Let the mixture simmer 20-25 minutes.Mixture will thicken slightly.Add hot sauce to taste.

• Add mixture to a plate and add a scoop of cooked white rice.

• Garnish with parsley and green onions and enjoy!

Blackberry Cobber

Blackberry Cobbler is a Classic Southern dessert with a buttery crust over warm bubbly tart fresh blackberries for the ultimate treat when served with ice cream.

Ingredients

• 2 cups all-purpose flour

• 1 tablespoon baking powder

• 3 tablespoons sugar

• ½ teaspoon salt

• ¼ teaspoon ground cinnamon

• ¼ teaspoon ground nutmeg

• 6 tablespoons cold unsalted butter, cubed

• ¾ cup heavy cream

• 6 cups fresh blackberries

• ½ cup sugar

• 1 tablespoon cornstarch

• 1 tablespoon lemon zest

• Heavy cream for brushing

• Cinnamon sugar for dusting

Instructions

• Preheat the oven to 350 degrees F. and butter a 9-inch deep-dish pie plate.

• In a medium bowl, whisk together the flour, baking powder, 3 tablespoons sugar, salt, cinnamon, and nutmeg until combined.

• Using a pastry blender or your hands, add the butter to the flour mixture and blend the butter into the flour mixture until the butter is pea-sized and the flour resembles a coarse meal.

• Pour ¾ cup heavy cream over the flour mixture and stir until it forms a soft dough and is fully combined. The dough will be soft and sticky, do not overwork or it will be tough.

• Turn the dough out onto a sheet of plastic wrap or wax paper and cover with another sheet.

• Use a rolling pin to gently roll the dough into a 9-inch round.Place the dough on a baking sheet, covered with plastic wrap, and place in the refrigerator while preparing the blackberry filling.

• In a large bowl, make the filling by gently stirring together the blackberries, ½ cup sugar, cornstarch, and lemon zest until mixed together.

• Pour the filling into the prepared pie plate.

• Remove the chilled dough from the refrigerator and cut a 2-inch wide hole in the center with a cookie cutter to create a steam vent.

• Place the dough on top of the blackberry filling and brush lightly with heavy cream and sprinkle with cinnamon sugar.

• Bake for 55 to 60 minutes, until the top is golden and the fruit is bubbling.Transfer to a wire rack and cool for 30 minutes before serving.

• Serve the blackberry cobbler warm with a scoop of your favorite ice cream. Refrigerate any unused portion up to 3 days

Makes 12 Servings

Apple Crisp

This is a quick and easy alternative to apple pie.Use any variety of apples that you have on hand

Ingredients

• 4 large baking apples, peeled and sliced

• ¾ cup brown sugar

• ½ cup flour

• ¾ cup oatmeal

• ¾ teaspoons cinnamon

• ½ cup reduced fat margarine

Instructions

• Heat oven to 350 degrees.

• Spray a baking pan with non-stick cooking spray and place apples into the pan. Mix sugar, flour, oatmeal and cinnamon in a bowl and place on top of apples.

• Drop dots of margarine on dry mixture. Bake for 25 minutes.

Makes 6 servings

Chicken Gumbo

This easy to make dish helps increase the amount of vegetables you eat and can be made in the same pot

Ingredients

• 1 tsp vegetable oil

• 1/4 cup flour

• 3 cups low-sodium chicken broth

• 1 1/2 lbs chicken breast, skinless and boneless, cut into 1-inch strips

• 1 cup white potatoes (1/2 lb), cubed 1 cup onions, chopped

• 1 cup carrots (1/2 lb), coarsely chopped

• 1/4 cup celery, chopped

• 1/2 medium carrot, grated 4 cloves garlic, finely minced

• 2 stalks scallion, chopped

• 1 whole bay leaf

• 1/2 tsp thyme

• 1/2 tsp black pepper, ground

• 2 tsps hot (or jalapeño) pepper

• 1 cup okra (1/2 lb), sliced into 1/2-inch pieces

Instructions

• Add oil to a large pot.

• Heat pot over medium flame.

• Stir in flour.

• Cook, stirring constantly, until flour begins to turn golden brown.

• Slowly stir in all the broth using a wire whisk and cook for 2 minutes.The mixture should not be lumpy.

• Add all ingredients except okra. Bring to a boil, then reduce heat and let simmer for 20 to 30 minutes.

• Add okra and let cook for 15 to 20 more minutes.

• Remove bay leaf.

• Serve hot in a bowl or over rice.

Makes 8 Servings

Jamaican jerk chicken

Ingredients

- 1/2 tsp cinnamon, ground
- 1 1/2 tsps allspice, ground
- 1 1/2 tsps black pepper, ground
- 1 Tbsp hot pepper, chopped
- 1 tsp hot pepper, crushed, dried
- 2 tsps oregano, crushed
- 2 tsps thyme, crushed
- 1/2 tsp salt
- 6 cloves garlic, finely chopped
- 1 cup onion, puréed or finely chopped
- 1/4 cup vinegar
- 3 Tbsps brown sugar
- 8 pieces chicken, skinless (4 breasts, 4 drumsticks)

Instructions

- Preheat oven to 350° F.

• Combine all ingredients except chicken in large bowl. Rub seasoning over chicken.

• Marinate in the refrigerator for 6 or more hours.

• Evenly space chicken on nonstick or lightly greased baking pan.

• Cover with aluminum foil and bake 40 minutes. Remove foil and continue baking for an additional 30 to 40 minutes or until the meat can be easily pulled away from the bone with a fork. The drumsticks may require less cooking time than the breasts.

Makes 6 Servings

Crispy oven-fried chicken

Ingredients

• 1/2 cup skim milk or buttermilk

• 1 tsp poultry seasoning

• 1 cup cornflakes, crumbled

• 1 1/2 Tbsps onion powder

• 1 1/2 Tbsps garlic powder

• 2 tsps black pepper

• 2 tsps dried hot pepper, crushed

• 1 tsp ginger, ground

• 8 pieces chicken, skinless (4 breasts, 4 drumsticks)

• A few shakes paprika

• 1 tsp vegetable oil (use to grease baking pan)

Instructions

• Preheat oven to 350° F.

• Add 1/2 teaspoon of poultry seasoning to milk.

• Combine all other spices with cornflake crumbs and place in a plastic bag.

• Wash chicken and pat dry.Dip chicken into milk, shake to remove excess, then quickly shake in bag with seasoning and crumbs.

• Refrigerate for 1 hour.

• Remove from refrigerator and sprinkle lightly with paprika for color.

• Evenly space chicken on greased baking pan.

• Cover with aluminum foil and bake 40 minutes. Remove foil and continue baking for an additional 30 to 40 minutes or until the meat can be easily pulled away from the bone with a fork.The drumsticks may require less baking time than the breasts. Crumbs will form a crispy "skin." (Do not turn chicken during baking.)

Spicy southern barbecued chicken

Instructions

• 5 Tbsps tomato paste (3 ozs)

• 1 tsp ketchup 2 tsps honey

• 1 tsp molasses

• 1 tsp Worcestershire sauce

• 4 tsps vinegar, white

• 3/4 tsp cayenne pepper

• 1/8 tsp black pepper

• 1/4 tsp onion powder

• 2 cloves garlic, minced

• 1/8 tsp ginger, grated

• 1 1/2 lbs chicken, skinless (breasts, drumsticks)

Instructions

• Combine all ingredients except chicken in a saucepan.

• Simmer for 15 minutes.

• Wash chicken and pat dry.

• Place chicken on a large platter.

• Brush chicken with 1/2 of sauce mixture.

• Cover with plastic wrap and marinate in refrigerator for 1 hour.

• Place chicken on a baking sheet lined with aluminum foil and broil for 10 minutes on each side to seal in juices.

• Turn oven down to 350° F, and add the remaining sauce to the chicken.

- Cover the chicken with aluminum foil and continue baking for 30 minutes.

www.ingramcontent.com/pod-product-compliance
Ingram Content Group UK Ltd.
Pitfield, Milton Keynes, MK11 3LW, UK
UKHW021654190726
13853UKWH00001B/259

9 798508 097004